**NEA
EARLY CHILDHOOD
EDUCATION SERIES**

Activity-
Oriented
Classrooms

WITHDRAWN

Milly Cowles
Jerry Aldridge

**A NATIONAL EDUCATION ASSOCIATION
PUBLICATION**

Printing History
    First Printing: March 1992

Note

The opinions expressed in this publication should not be construed as representing the policy or position of the National Education Association. Materials published by the NEA Professional Library are intended to be discussion documents for educators who are concerned with specialized interests of the profession.

All trademarks and registered trademarks depicted in this book belong to their respective holders.

Library of Congress Cataloging-in-Publication Data

Cowles, Milly.
    Activity-oriented classrooms / Milly Cowles, Jerry Aldridge.
        p.   cm. —(NEA early childhood education series)
    Includes bibliographical references (p.).
    ISBN 0–8106–0352–7
    1. Early childhood education—United States—Activity programs—
Handbooks, manuals, etc. 2. Teaching—Aids and devices—Handbooks,
manuals, etc. I. Aldridge, Jerry. II. Title. III. Series.
LB1139.35.A37C69   1992
372.13'078—dc20   91–8549
                                                      CIP

CONTENTS

The Authors

Milly Cowles is Distinguished Professor Emerita of Early Childhood Education, School of Education, University of Alabama at Birmingham.

Jerry Aldridge is Associate Professor of Curriculum and Instruction, School of Education, University of Alabama at Birmingham.

The Advisory Panel

David Bell, Professor of Education, Arkansas Tech University, Russellville

Barbara Blanchard, Kindergarten Teacher, Somerville, Massachusetts

Patricia R. Gwaltney, Elementary Resource Teacher, Pike County School Corporation, Petersburg, Indiana

Diane Kelley, Kindergarten Teacher, Grant Elementary School, Spokane, Washington

Karen Lewis, Kindergarten Teacher, Lincoln Elementary School, West Chicago, Illinois

Sharon Morgan, Kindergarten Teacher, Raymond Gabaldon Elementary School, Los Lunas, New Mexico

Chapter 1

INTRODUCTION

The educational environment is the most important place for children other than their homes. Indeed, after beginning school, children spend more time with teachers and classmates than with their families. Teachers know that their influence and the impact of the educational environment have lasting, positive values. Unfortunately, in recent years, there has been an enormous pressure to require educators to standardize the curriculum and place young children in the middle of activities that prepare them to score better on standardized tests. The great masses of research and informed opinion have shown that for continued success both in school and in later life, however, the majority of children perform much better in a personalized and individualized educational environment. There are many reasons why such classrooms and educational practices are most appropriate. They include the following:

1. *Children learn by doing.* Children learn through active participation and involvement. Exploring the environment, using manipulative materials, experiencing concrete, hands-on activities through individual participation and social interaction are ways that young children coordinate relationships and construct their own knowledge.

2. *Children learn from the concrete to the semiconcrete to the abstract.* This concept can be demonstrated by the way children learn about apples. If we want children to learn about an apple, we engage them in concrete activities with the actual object. They taste, touch, and smell the apple and then make applesauce, apple butter, or other products. Semiconcrete activities often use pictures or picture representations of objects. Drawing pictures of apples, counting the number of apples in a

picture or looking at representations of apples in books are semiconcrete activities. Finally, children eventually develop abstract concepts about apples. They learn that apple starts with the letter "a" and that they can write the word "apple" or read recipes for an apple salad. In activity-oriented classrooms children have opportunities to explore the environment at a concrete level before moving on to semiconcrete and abstract representations of concepts.

3. *Children need a balance between teacher-initiated activities and child-initiated activities.* Activity-oriented classrooms are not just teacher-directed, their activities are also student-initiated. This is a very important balance in these classrooms because of the types of knowledge described by Piaget. Piaget believed that children acquire *social knowledge, physical knowledge,* and *logical-mathematical knowledge.* Teacher-initiated activities are one way that children gain social knowledge—knowledge learned from someone else. Names of objects and people are often learned from the teacher. Children cannot construct social knowledge from just exploring the environment. For example, the fact that George Washington was the first president of the United States is something they can learn from teacher-directed information. In early childhood activity-oriented classrooms the teacher can consider that children learn from the concrete to the semiconcrete to the abstract when preparing activities for social knowledge. Physical knowledge is sometimes learned through child-initiated activities. Through exploration of concrete objects, children experiment and construct the properties concerning the objects through hands-on learning. They develop logical-mathematical knowledge through classifying, sorting, and categorizing objects such as apples (34).*

---

*Numbers in parentheses appearing in the text refer to the Bibliography beginning on page 77.

4. *Children learn from individually exploring the environment and through social interactions.* Just as activity-oriented classrooms need a balance between teacher-directed and child-initiated activities, they also need a balance between individual and group activities. This is important for personality reasons as well as cognitive ones. Some children are introverts and prefer activities that allow individual exploration, while others are more extroverted and enjoy group interaction. Children learn from the two types of activities. The activity-oriented classroom includes both kinds.

5. *Children need an inviting, friendly, and safe physical environment.* A classroom should provide an inviting and friendly place for children. Activity-oriented classrooms are composed of learning centers with books, dramatic play, puzzles, games, science activities, art and music equipment, and other inviting materials. Many manipulatives exist in these classrooms and the schedule of daily events is inviting in that it provides a balance, not only of teacher- and child-initiated activities and individual and group learning, but also of active and quiet periods.

6. *Children learn at different rates.* An effective classroom provides for differing rates of learning. Children who are actively engaged in exploring can move at an individual pace with support from the teacher. An activity-oriented classroom allows for individual differences and uses cooperative learning and peer tutoring.

7. *Children need to explore their specific types of intelligences.* Activity-oriented classrooms allow teachers to ask the question, "How is this child smart?" rather than "How smart is this child?" Howard Gardner's theory of multiple intelligences holds that children have specific types of intelligence such as musical or linguistic (14). Developmentally appropriate classrooms allow children to explore the areas they enjoy and the areas in which they have specific talents.

This publication is divided into six chapters. The Introduction (Chapter 1) has given an overview of activity-oriented classrooms. Chapters 2–4 describe how to design an activity-oriented classroom for individual and group learning. Chapter 2 explains how to set up an activity-oriented classroom; Chapters 3 and 4 discuss individually oriented activities and group-oriented instruction, respectively. Chapter 5 illustrates activity-oriented learning with examples in art, reading and language arts, mathematics, science, and social studies. While we recommend teaching through integrated units in an activity-oriented classroom, Chapter 5 provides ideas for using content areas that can be integrated into units. Chapter 6 concludes with additional suggestions for curriculum planning and evaluation.

Chapter 2

SETTING UP THE ACTIVITY-ORIENTED CLASSROOM

Activity-oriented classrooms in grades K-3 are best implemented if the administration is convinced, involved, and supportive of the underlying philosophy. Further, activity-based instruction is more successful when parents are involved and when the class environment is planned to accommodate movement and exploration. This is often accomplished through various types of learning stations with developmentally appropriate games and activities. In other words, designing and implementing an activity-focused room can be both rewarding and enjoyable for teachers who (1) plan programs with the administration, (2) enlist the help of parents from the beginning, (3) prepare the environment for active learning, (4) develop an activity-oriented schedule, (5) create learning stations, and (6) construct games and activities that are child-centered.

PLANNING PROGRAMS WITH THE ADMINISTRATION

Activity-focused classrooms are more successful with administrative support. School principals are more helpful when they understand the underlying philosophy behind such classrooms. Activity-oriented classrooms are based on developmentally appropriate practice, which is concerned with how children learn, what they learn, how to measure what they learn, and the overall aims of the education process. Elkind has compared developmentally appropriate practice with psychometric educational psychology, the most operational philosophy in today's schools: "No classroom or school can truly be developmentally appropriate if its underlying philosophy is psychometric" (13, p.

11

117). The first task in implementing an activity-focused classroom, then, is to work with the administration and engage the principal in valuing developmentally appropriate practice.

How do teachers go about convincing principals to support efforts at activity-driven learning? This is extremely challenging since it may involve a shift in current attitudes and assessment practices. These changes take time to develop. Teachers can make a start, though, by (1) discussing the activity-oriented classroom with the principal and enlisting help in designing the program, and (2) working with the principal to construct a teacher evaluation system that reflects activity-based instruction.

Developing the activity-based classroom with the principal. Teachers can start by preparing an outline or action plan for initiating an activity-focused program. The major components of the plan of action should include (1) explaining the philosophy, (2) developing a procedure, and (3) implementing an accountability system. Suggestions for the underlying philosophy of activity-based classrooms can be found in Bredekamp's *Developmentally Appropriate Practice in Early Childhood Programs Serving Children from Birth Through Age 8* (6). An outline of procedures is developed throughout this publication. Finally, an accountability system refers to how the effectiveness of activity-focused instructional programs is measured. This can be accomplished in part by working with the administration on an evaluation system that is designed to reflect activity-oriented classrooms.

Constructing a teacher evaluation system that reflects the activity-based classrooms. The last thing most teachers want is another evaluation form. Since developmentally appropriate classrooms have different goals and procedures from those based on traditional psychometric educational psychology, however, their success should be measured differently. Table 2.1 gives an example of a teacher evaluation checklist that was developed for use in developmentally appropriate, active learning environments.

Table 2.1
Kindergarten-Primary
Teacher Evaluation Checklist

Developmentally appropriate elements in Early Childhood Education classrooms. Check whether or not items are observed.

	Observed	Not Observed
Physical Environment/Atmosphere		
1. Inviting	———	———
2. Friendly	———	———
Learning Centers		
1. Book	———	———
2. Language Arts	———	———
3. Dramatic Play/Social Studies	———	———
4. Block/Small Builders	———	———
5. Puzzles/Games	———	———
6. Science	———	———
7. Art	———	———
Equipment/Materials		
1. Many manipulatives	———	———
2. Reflect curriculum goals for grade	———	———
Organization		
1. Plans include:		
a. teacher-directed activities	———	———
b. activities that children choose	———	———
2. Plans reflect different kinds of grouping:		
a. whole group	———	———
b. small group	———	———
c. one-to-one		
3. Schedule has balance:		
a. active/quiet	———	———
b. individual/interactive	———	———

Table 2.1 (Continued)

	Observed	Not Observed
Adult-Child Interactive		
1. Interacts frequently with students	———	———
2. Attends to large-group, small-group, and individual needs	———	———
3. Involves children with concrete hands-on activities	———	———
4. Uses a limited number of work-sheets, drills, and sitting/listening activities	———	———
5. Uses integrated curriculum	———	———
6. Avoids use of fragmented short, 15- to 20-minute periods with lecture, worksheet, and drill	———	———

ENLISTING THE HELP OF PARENTS

Activity-oriented classrooms are most in need of parental support. Parents can be encouraged not only to lend moral support but also to design and help with materials. The following are suggestions for enlisting help from parents:

1. At the first parents' meeting of the school year, explain the activity-focused classroom:
   a. why it is important for children to be active learners
   b. how the activity-based program works
   c. what children do in learning stations
   d. how children are evaluated in the program
   e. how parents can help with the program.
2. Ask for parent volunteers.
3. Send progress reports of the program to parents throughout the year.
4. Keep student activity products and share them frequently with parents.
5. Evaluate the progress of the program with parents during individual conferences and at later parents' meetings during the year.

PREPARING THE ENVIRONMENT

Ideally, the activity-enriched class is one with large amounts of space with children working from tables and learning stations instead of desks. Separate classroom learning stations would be prepared for art and music, reading and language arts, mathematics, science, dramatization/social studies, computer(s), blocks/small builders or woodworking, and a multipurpose station that might include puzzles and games. Chapter 5 provides descriptions of most of these stations. A sample classroom diagram appears in Figure 2.1 (9).

Table 2.1
Sample Diagram of a Classroom

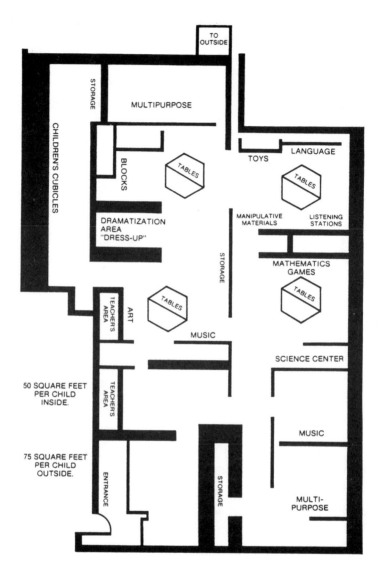

Source: Milly Cowles, *Quality Early Childhood Education in the South* (Decatur, Ga.: Commission on Elementary Schools, Southern Association of Colleges and Schools, 1990).

16

DEVELOPING AN ACTIVITY-ORIENTED SCHEDULE

There are many ways to develop a daily schedule in an activity-based setting. Certain guidelines may be helpful. According to Eddowes and Aldridge,

> There is a need for balance between teacher-initiated large-group and child-initiated small-group activities. Large-group activities can follow the double-the-age rule—small-group and individual activities should not. The small-group activities and individual exploration time periods should be extended to from 45 minutes to one hour or more, depending upon available activities. (12)

Table 2.2 contains a list of suggested activities for developing a schedule that balances teacher-initiated large-group and child-initiated small-group activities.

CREATING LEARNING STATIONS

Learning stations were very popular in the 1960s and 1970s but were often perceived as difficult to manage or controversial. This was due in part to development problems. To maximize their effectiveness and manageability, learning stations or centers should be constructed in a systematic fashion.

There are three major guidelines for setting up a learning station. First, start with only one center and teach a lesson on how to use it. Learning stations do not run themselves without careful planning and explanation. Second, explain to children the goal, procedures, and accountability system of the learning station. Children need to be told the purposes of the center, the ways and steps to go about using it, and how to meet accountability. Accountability is a very important aspect of the learning center. Students must demonstrate in some way that they did something there. If accountability is not present or

17

Table 2.2
Suggested Activities for Developing a
Balanced Schedule

Large-Group Activities	Small-Group Activities
(Short Time Periods)	(Long Blocks of Time)
Weather	Comparing/Classifying/ Sorting/Matching
Finger Plays	Building with Blocks
Planning the Day	Role Playing/Dramatization
Daily News	Working with Pegs/Beads/ Puzzles
Listening to Stories	Painting/Art Media
Singing	Looking at Books/Puppets
Music/Movement	Individual Games
Group Games	
Sharing	

Source: E. Anne Eddowes, and Jerry Aldridge, "Hyperactive or 'Activity Hyper': Helping Young Children Attend in Appropriate Environments," *Day Care and Early Education* 17, no. 4 [Summer 1990]: 29–32.

required, students may not work appropriately at the station. Third, do not create a second learning center until the first one is working well, and do not move to a third center until the second one is working smoothly. How can a teacher manage eight learning stations if he/she cannot manage one?

Good learning centers have seven characteristics: (1) clear instructions, (2) clear objectives, (3) a choice provided, (4) multilevel activities, (5) self-corrective materials, (6) manipulatives, and (7) small-group as well as individual activities (35). Creating learning stations takes considerable planning. Active help from the children in designing and constructing the stations can be valuable.

CONSTRUCTING CHILD-CENTERED GAMES AND ACTIVITIES

The most important consideration in developing activities is the child. The curriculum and activities should be based on the child's needs as well as the curriculum demands. Because the activities should be based on the child's needs, it is difficult to describe games and activities that would meet every child's needs. However, there are some generic game and activity patterns that can be used for many subjects, skills, and needs. These include (1) car wheels, (2) tachistoscopes, (3) seek and peek, (4) minipuzzles, (5) self-corrective stars, (6) wheel-pattern activities, and (7) milk carton self-corrective activities. Chapter 3 describes these activity patterns.

Chapter 3

INDIVIDUALLY ORIENTED ACTIVITIES

Chapter 3 is divided into two sections. The first section answers the question, "Why should individually oriented activities be a part of an activities-based curriculum?" The second section describes generic activity patterns that can be adapted for individual needs.

THE IMPORTANCE OF INDIVIDUALLY ORIENTED ACTIVITIES

An important question to be addressed is, "Why should teachers develop individually focused activities and games in an active learning environment?" There are seven reasons why individually oriented activities are necessary. All refer to individuality among children. They involve differences in ecology, topology, learning rates, learning styles, types of intelligence, special needs, and self-esteem.

Differences in ecology. Children need individual activities because they come from diverse environments. Some children are read to at home and may be ready for abstract learning by second and third grade. Others come from less enriching backgrounds and may need more concrete activities. Changes in the economy, family structure, and overall ecology have increased both interindividual and intraindividual differences, creating a need for more one-on-one instruction (7).

Differences in typology. Children are also different in their temperament. Individual activities are important for emotional as well as cognitive reasons. Both introverts and extroverts require time to reflect on their learning. Individualization is important for personality differences (3).

Differences in learning rates. Not only is there diversity in learning rates among children, but within the same child there is variance in learning. A child may be extremely adept at mathematics but much slower in reading development. Individual activities can be used in activity-focused classes to capitalize on individual strengths and to lessen weaknesses (30).

Differences in learning styles. Children vary in the ways they take in information and in their time of day preferences for learning. Some children are kinesthetic learners, while others may be auditory or visual learners. There are many dimensions to an individual's learning style that require specific attention (11).

Differences in types of intelligence. The old saying "No one is good at everything, but everyone is good at something" is true. Individual exploration of talents is important for children to discover their uniqueness. Among the many different types of intelligence are mathematical, linguistic, visual-spatial, bodily-kinesthetic, interpersonal, intrapersonal, and artistic. These can be explored through individual activities. An artist does not learn to paint by attending to mathematics (14).

Differences in special needs. In addition to diversities in learning rates and styles, and types of intelligence, learners can also have other differences such as physical handicaps. These children may need occupational or physical therapy. Teachers who provide time for individual development can help orthopedically handicapped children, for example, by allowing for activities related to occupational or physical therapy (30).

Differences in self-esteem. The development of self-esteem in young children is crucial. This can be partially accomplished by attending to and valuing the preceding differences. Requirements of high self-esteem include a sense of belonging, a feeling of individuality, the opportunity to choose, and the presence of good models (1). All four of these requirements are addressed through individually appropriate activities.

INDIVIDUAL GAME PATTERNS

One way to meet individual needs is through games. Chapter 2 introduced seven generic game patterns. Certain cautions must be mentioned for constructing and using these games. First, these patterns tend to reinforce skills in isolation. Second, these games are mostly suited for matching activities. Anything that cannot be matched cannot be used. Third, the games are time-consuming to construct. These disadvantages can be partially overcome by allowing children to help design and make the games. Second and third graders are more likely to be able to help in constructing these resources than are kindergartners or first graders.

Car Wheels. Car wheels can be used for any type of matching activity in language arts, mathematics, science, or social studies. The student places all matching items on top of the wheels, as shown in the illustration.

Seek and Peek. Seek and peek games can also be developed for matching. An example of a seek-and-peek activity for spelling would be to paste a picture of a spelling word on an index card with a selection of several spellings at the bottom and a hole punched beneath each word choice. The correct spelling is marked on the back with a highlighter. Students put their pencils through the hole beneath their selection. They can check the answer on the back of the card.

cat   hat   bat

$3 + 2 =$

4   5   6   7

Tachistoscopes. Tachistocopes can be developed for any content area subject. One use for them is with word patterns as shown in the example that follows. Two movable portions can be used for designing mathematics problem games.

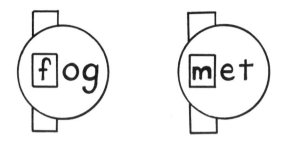

Minipuzzles. Index cards can be used to develop minipuzzles. For example, for a spelling minipuzzle game, blends, digraphs, and word beginnings or endings can be matched in the minipuzzle format. Or pictures can be matched with a word written in standard manuscript. Only one correct answer should be possible, however, or students will become confused.

Self-Corrective Stars. Activities can be made with star points to be matched to a centerpiece. Place several cut-up stars in one envelope.

Milk Carton Matching Game. Self-corrective activities can be made by using a half-gallon paper milk carton. First, cover the milk carton with contact paper; then, attach any type of matching game to it.

Pizza-Wheel Activities. Pizza boards (wheels) and clothespins can be used to make any type of matching wheel game. See the illustration matching pictures of products with their names.

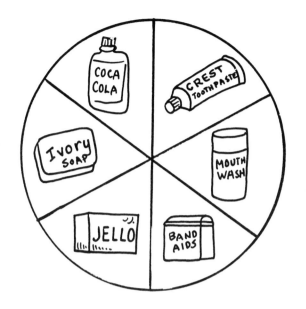

Chapter 4

GROUP-ORIENTED CLASSROOMS

Just as children learn through individual activities, they also benefit from group work. There are many advantages to group-oriented classrooms. For example, children learn from each other while they share and coordinate ideas. This can occur through many types of grouping and group activities.

Children learn from each other. Sometimes the best teachers are other children. Adults can forget how difficult it was to learn certain concepts. Children who are constructing their own knowledge may be able to better explain material because they can remember the problems or pitfalls they have just encountered in learning a particular skill. Children and adults are also on different cognitive levels. This is another advantage for group learning, since children think more like each other than they do like adults.

Children learn by sharing and coordinating relationships. Social interactions are important for the construction of knowledge. For example, if three children are working on the math problem "2 + 3 = ____ ," they benefit from sharing with each other how they came up with their answers. If one child arrived at the answer "4" while the others decided on "5," all will understand the process better if they are asked to explain to each other how they arrived at their answers. Hopefully, by sharing and coordinating their ideas, the student who constructed "4" will discover the error in reasoning (22).

Children learn through different types of grouping. There are two basic types of grouping: homogenous (grouping those who are alike), and heterogeneous (grouping those who are different). Within each of these two types of group are a multitude of organizational possibilities for activity-focused classes. Specific types of grouping include achievement groups, special needs or skills groups, interest groups, research groups,

29

friendship groups, pupil partners, peer tutoring, and mixed-age grouping.

SPECIFIC TYPES OF GROUPS

Achievement Groups. Children who achieve at a similar level, often determined by a standardized test score, are sometimes placed in homogenous achievement groups. This method of organization may not be appropriate for activity-based learning. Achievement groups are more often used in traditional psychometric-based rooms for reading and mathematics. Students who spend long periods of time in these groups may not benefit as much from other children as they might in other grouping patterns. For example, Allen reports that poor readers in achievement groups are subjected to learning to read by listening to other poor readers read poorly (5). Further, children who spend large amounts of time in achievement groups may suffer from low self-esteem, particularly if they are in the lowest group. Children are usually aware of such placement.

Special Needs or Skills Groups. Another homogenous grouping strategy, the special needs group, is composed of children who need work on the same skill. Such groups are often used with the individualized reading approach (25). Children are grouped for particular skills, and as skills are mastered the groups change frequently.

Interest Groups. Children who share a common interest may work in this type of group. For example, in an activity-focused class, students who enjoy bear stories may work together to read and share bear stories and write about them. This approach is also effective for activity-oriented science and social studies.

Research Groups. These groups are made up of children with varying abilities who work together to investigate a special topic. The group may research any content area. Members can work together to determine the origins of certain foods (science) or proper dental care (health), for example.

Friendship Groups. Both an informal and formal purpose can be served through this grouping pattern. Friends work together to complete a task within a specified time.

Pupil Partners. Some activity-focused rooms use pupil pairs to work on the same project. The pairs may be homogenous or heterogeneous. The partners can be engaged in any of the preceding types of activities, such as an interest or research group composed of two members.

Peer Tutoring. Peer tutoring programs have the same three requirements as those of a good learning center or station: (1) a goal, (2) a procedure, and (3) an accountability system. Peer tutoring can take many forms—for example: (1) a brighter student helping a slower student, (2) cross-age tutoring with a second or third grader helping a kindergartner or first grader, and (3) three-way peer tutoring with three students in the class who have the same need.

The most common type of peer tutoring is designed for a bright child to help a less-able student. This most often occurs within the same classroom. The disadvantage of this method is that the slower child never becomes a tutor.

Cross-age tutoring can be designed to encourage an older, less-able student to help a younger child. A third grader who is recruited to help a first grader with reading benefits from the process because the older, less-able student must practice reading to the first grader. He/she also benefits in improved self-esteem. There are obvious advantages for the first grader as well.

Harris and Aldridge have developed a peer tutoring plan that can be used with special needs learners. Their program groups three children who have the same need. After the children are selected, they are trained to be tutors. As a group, the three students make their own games and decide on the rules with the teacher's help. The job of tutor changes among the three students every session. One student is tutor one day and another the next day. Activity-oriented learning is the basis of the model, with all three children sharing roles and responsibilities for group games (17).

Mixed-Age Grouping. Mixed-age grouping can be formal or informal. The ungraded primary school is an example of a permanent, more formal mixed-age system, while class partnerships (such as a third grade and kindergarten class working together occasionally) are more informal. Katz, Evangelou, and Hartman have described the cognitive and social benefits of mixed-age settings (23).

Chapter 5

ACTIVITY-ORIENTED CONTENT

This chapter introduces activity-focused learning in art, reading and language arts, mathematics, science, and social studies. Activity-oriented content possibilities are limitless. This chapter is by no means comprehensive. It provides only a few examples for each area.

Developmentally appropriate practice was a strong consideration for activity-oriented classrooms. Developmentally appropriate practice includes both age-appropriate and individually appropriate activities (6). The activities that follow are designed for a wide range of abilities. Therefore, no specific ages are given, but each activity may be individually appropriate for children ages 5 though 8.

ACTIVITY-ORIENTED ART

Children are not born thinking they have no artistic ability. Unfortunately, many of them develop the attitude that they are not creative. Sometimes they learn this in school. An activity-focused art program allows children to explore various media and develop their own creations without developing negative attitudes about their abilities. Certain principles guide active participation in art.

1. *Encourage exploration and use of numerous and varied materials.* Art supplies would include finger paints, liquid or powdered tempera, paintbrushes, crayons, colored chalk, glue, paste, masking tape, clay, playdough, plasticene, computer paper, fabrics, wallpaper books, magazines, construction paper, Styrofoam, sandpaper, soap, and stickers (10). Teachers should foster active exploration of each type of media.

2. *Value free expression.* There is a difference between active expression of art and standard craft-making. Art expression is individually selected and carried out. Children choose and experience the different materials in developing a product of their own making. Craft activities are geared to following directions and producing standard, look-alike items. Children creating art have something individual to develop. The product, though, is never as important as the active, personal response.

3. *Use patterns, models, color sheets, and coloring books minimally, if at all.* To encourage free expression, activity-focused rooms limit the use of standard examples, models, or coloring activities. Coloring and patterning are more appropriate for fine motor development and have limited or no value in the creative process.

4. *Enjoy and display all children's creations.* There is no such thing as the "best" art work among kindergartners and primary graders. Individual contributions of each child can be shown on bulletin boards or school halls. This is not to say that all children will want their art work displayed. Unfortunately, primary graders may begin to feel that their artistic talent is inferior to that of another. A developmentally appropriate art program can do much to restore the confidence of these children by encouraging them to share their work, just as their mothers exhibit it on the refrigerator door.

5. *Encourage children to help prepare the media as well as use it.* One important aspect in active art rooms is that children make their own finger paints, easel paints, modeling clay, playdough, liquid paste, paper paste, and craft clay. Other content areas are enhanced when children follow recipes and see cause-effect relationships as they prepare the media for their expression. The following recipes are provided to help teachers elicit active participation in the preparation of materials.

Finger Paint
>   1 1/2 cups liquid soap (do not use detergent)
>   6 cups liquid starch (liquid starch can be made with 3
>   parts flour and 4 parts water)
>   food coloring

Mix the soap and liquid starch. Add the food coloring.

Easel Paint
>   1 cup powdered tempera
>   1/2 cup starch
>   1/2 cup liquid soap

Mix liquid soap and starch in a container. Stir tempera into mixture. Let stand for one hour or more. Stir again until all lumps are gone. Store in tightly covered plastic jars. Shake well before using.

Modeling Clay
>   2 3/4 cups cornstarch
>   4 cups sand (fine, medium, or coarse, depending on
>   texture desired)
>   3 1/2 cups hot water
>   4 teaspoons alum
>   food coloring (optional)

Mix sand, alum, and cornstarch. Gradually add hot water and cook over medium heat, stirring constantly, until mixture thickens. Add food coloring, if desired. Remove from heat and knead. Store in airtight containers or sealed plastic bags. Objects made from this material may be painted after they have dried.

Playdough
>   Heat oven to 250° F. Mix the following ingredients:
>   1 1/2 cups salt
>   6 cups flour
>   2 to 3 cups water

Bake up to 1 hour, depending on thickness desired. For a glossy effect, brush on some condensed milk before baking or use a mixture of condensed milk and food coloring.

Liquid Paste
     1 cup regular library paste
     8–12 tablespoons boiling water
Gradually add boiling water to library paste—small amounts at a time. Store in airtight containers.

Classroom Paste
     $1^1/2$ cups sugar
     6 cups boiling water
     $1^1/2$ cups wheat flour (non-self-rising)
     $1^1/2$ cups cold water
     $3/4$ teaspoon oil of wintergreen
Combine flour and sugar. Gradually add cold water. Slowly stir in boiling water. On medium heat, bring the solution to a boil. Stir constantly until mixture is thick and clear. Remove from heat. Add wintergreen and alum. Store in airtight containers.

Craft Clay
     $2^1/2$ cups water
     4 cups baking soda
     2 cups cornstarch
Mix baking soda and cornstarch and gradually add water, stirring until smooth. Cook over medium heat, stirring constantly until doughlike. Turn mixture on a pastry board and knead well. Store in plastic bag until needed. Roll out thin and cut in desired shapes or with a cookie cutter.

ACTIVITY-ORIENTED READING AND LANGUAGE ARTS

Beginning reading and writing are enhanced in active environments where teachers develop stories, letters, and words in a meaningful context that proceeds from the concrete to the abstract (4). Traditional reading and writing instruction can be supplemented and in some cases replaced with more activity-focused language approaches and games. Environmental print activities, the key words approach, the daily news, predictable books, big books, and the writing process are all examples of activity-based learning.

Environmental Print Activities

Young children learn from print in the environment. They learn from logos on candy bar wrappers, potato chip packages, food store bags, soft drink bottles or cans, and advertisements found in newspapers or magazines. Teachers can use and extend this knowledge by developing an activity-based print awareness program. The following suggestions are made for starting an environmental print program.

Step 1. Have students bring in wrappers, cans, advertisements, or any printed symbol they can find in their homes or neighborhood. Teachers can store these materials in a large box. During reading time, the teacher can take items from the box and ask children to identify them. "Who brought this wrapper? What does it say?"

Step 2. The teacher then photocopies the items in the box and shows the copies to the children at the next reading session. Children name the products in the photocopies.

Step 3. At the next reading session, the teacher and children write the product names on the board. Also, the teacher might write "Coke, for example," on the board and have children write the word and talk about its letters and sounds.

Step 4. Children and teacher then make up sentences and stories using the environmental print words.

Step 5. After children have been through the first four steps of the print awareness process, games and activities can be used to reinforce environmental print learning. These games need to stress the movement of children from steps 1 and 2 to steps 3 and 4. In other words, if a matching game is used, the student should be required to match one of the first two steps to one of the last two, since children have the most difficulty in making the transition to standard manuscript. Usually, children who recognize a logo can recognize a photocopy of it in any form (8). The real difficulty comes in recognizing products when they are written in a standard manuscript form. Some examples of environmental print games follow.

Box Top Match. A folder game can be devised with box tops from grocery store products that children have brought to class. Children match a card containing the product name written in standard manuscript with the appropriate box top attached to the folder. An example follows.

Bingo. Bingo cards can be developed with products and logos the children have collected. The teacher holds up a logo or product name written in standard manuscript and the children must find it on their card. (See the example below.)

Pop Top Lotto. Bottled soft drinks usually have the logo on the cap or top. Save these caps and make the game Pop Top Lotto. Children take the tops and match them to the logo square on a lotto board. An example follows.

Minipuzzles. Minipuzzles are easy to make from plain white index cards. The teacher can have students match steps 2, 3, and 4 of print awareness (see page 37), using the products they have brought to class. Examples follow.

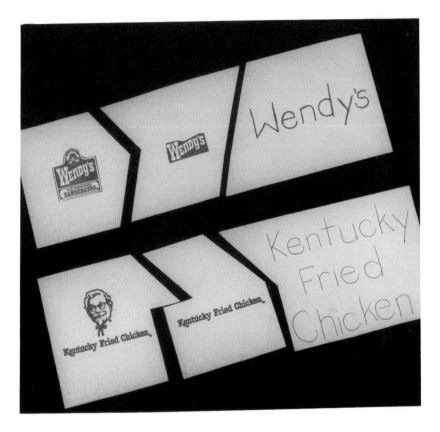

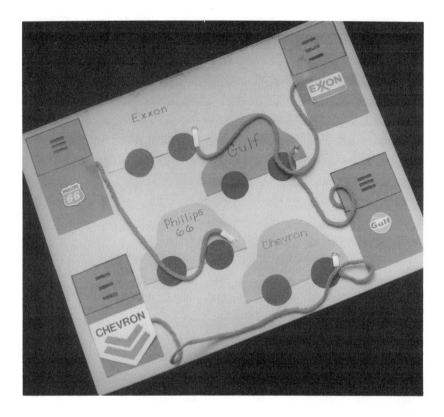

Fill It Up. Find logo symbols from various gas stations in the neighborhood of the school. Place these on gas pumps you have drawn. Make construction paper cars with the gas pump logo written in manuscript on the cars. Attach a piece of yarn to each gas pump and have students match the gas pump to the appropriate car. An example is given on the following page.

Grocery List. Have students bring food store advertising pages from the newspaper to class. Give each child one page with an index card attached with a paper clip. The index card should contain the names of several products from the advertisement, written in standard manuscript with a crayon the color of the product. The child is to circle the product in the advertisement using the crayon. An example is given on the following page.

Small Order of Fries. Have students bring to class french fry packages from local fast-food restaurants. Paste these to a folder to make the game Small Order of Fries. Make paper french fries from yellow construction paper and write in manuscript the name of a fast-food logo on each one. Ask students to match each french fry to the appropriate package. An example follows.

Logo Lace-Up. Collect logos of neighborhood stores. Paste them in a column on the left side of a sheet of poster board or cardboard. Have students match each store's logo to the appropriate store name written in manuscript in a second column. This game can be made easy by punching holes next to the written words and taping yarn next to the logo. Students place the yarn in the hole next to the manuscript word that matches the logo. An example follows. (Note: Wrap the tip of the yarn with masking tape so that children can easily punch through the hole next to the written word that matches the logo.)

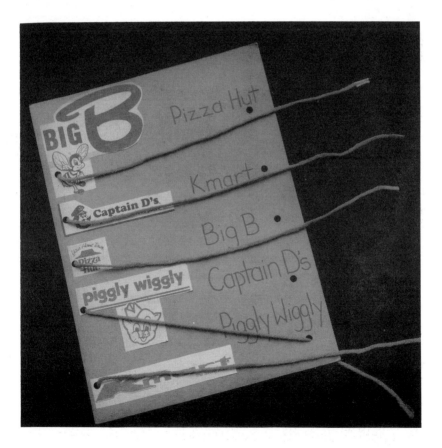

Alpha Bit Print. Paste common logos to index cards, one logo per card. Place a package of dry cereal that uses alphabet pieces into a sealed food package. Students are to take the alphabet pieces and spell the word on the card beneath the logo. Then, they can eat the words they have spelled. An example follows.

Logo Lotto. Paste logos to poster board, cardboard, or a folder in two columns. Write the logos in standard manuscript on separate index cards. Ask children to match the manuscript cards to the logos on the board. An example is given on the following page.

Logo Reading. Use two sets of index cards. On the first set, place one logo on each card. On the second set, write sentences (one per card), using the logos from the first set. Ask children to match the logo with the card containing the sentence that uses the logo. Examples of cards follow.

Alphabet Gobblers. Make an animal figure for each letter of the alphabet. (Usually grocery store coloring books contain animal alphabet figures.) Find logos beginning with each letter of the alphabet. Cut a place in the mouth of each animal for the children to place logos that begin with the first letter of the animal's name. Then, make cards with the logos (one per card) for the children to feed the alphabet gobblers (for example, for a kangaroo, Kentucky Fried Chicken). This activity can be placed on the bulletin board and the whole room can be covered with alphabet gobblers if the teacher chooses to do so. A small paper bag or pouch can be attached on the back of the alphabet gobbler to catch what the animal is "fed." An example follows.

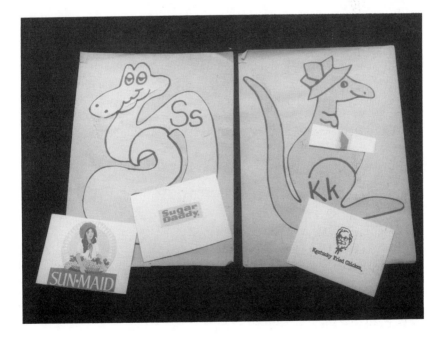

What's Missing? Place a logo on a piece of construction paper. Write the word below the logo in standard manuscript, omitting one letter. Students have to determine which letter is missing and place the letter in the appropriate space. (Alphabet letters can be written individually on small squares for children to choose.) An example follows.

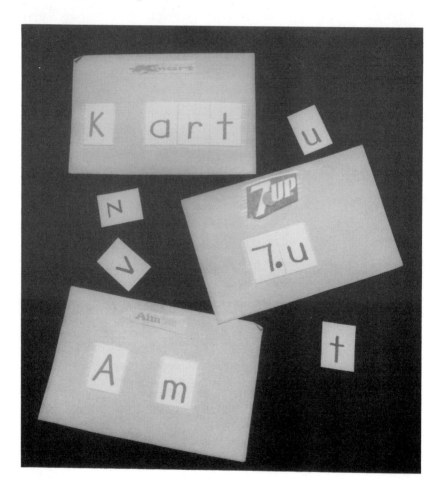

Logo Alphabet Books. Alphabet books can be made of logos. Each student can have an "A" page, a "B" page, etc. As students find logos in the neighborhood, they can paste them on the appropriate alphabet page. An example follows.

My Favorite Logo. Children bring to class logos of their favorite products. Each child pastes a logo on one side of a piece of art paper. Then, he or she draws a picture opposite the logo and writes a sentence about the favorite logo below the drawing. These pages can be combined to form a book. An example is given on the following page.

The Key Words Approach

The key words approach is an activity-based program that uses the child's own language and experiences. It gives the child an opportunity to acquire an individual collection of words (33).

There are several guidelines for using the key words approach:

1. Each day, ask every child to give you a word. Ask such questions as, "What word would you like me to write for you?"
2. Print the word on an index card or a sentence strip with a marker. Have the child stand by your shoulder or sit next to you so that she or he does not look at the word upside down. Ask the child to name the letters as you print them.
3. Have the child trace the printing with a finger.
4. Then ask the child to do an activity with the word—draw a picture of it, write it on the blackboard, or any other activity he/she chooses.
5. Once a week have children bring their words to you and review them.
6. When storage of children's words becomes a problem, make individual folders for each child, or have children make a ring file by punching holes in their word cards and placing them on a plastic or metal ring.

The Daily News Approach

The daily news is an effective way to start the day and plan the day's activities with the children. With the help of students, the teacher writes the day, the date, the weather report, and the activities plan.

For example:

The Daily News

Today is Monday, October 5, 1992. It is sunny and cool outside. We will experiment with magnets during Science. During Social Studies we will play our favorite community helpers. We will use dice games during math.

Predictable Books

Predictable books are literary works that contain at least one of these patterns: (1) a familiar sequence, (2) repetition, or (3) a cumulative pattern (26). Children's active participation is encouraged because they are asked to read the repetitive part of the book together. Children can make their own predictable books based on the pattern of a predictable book they have read. A list of predictable books appears in the Appendix.

Big Books

Big books are used to stimulate the bedtime story experience with the entire class. The whole class is an active participant in the reading and sharing of the story (20). The following suggestions will make big book reading even more activity-oriented:

1. Read the story aloud to the class.
2. Read the story again and point to each word.
3. Reread the story inviting the children to help with the reading.
4. Dramatize parts of the story.
5. At the next reading, read up to the last word of a particular sentence and pause for children to supply the missing word.
6. Repeat step 5 several times, leaving out other words.

7. Write the story on the chalkboard, overhead, or flip-chart for children to read. (Children will see the story written in another form.)
8. Point out the concept of letters, words, phrases, and punctuation found in the story.
9. Have the children listen to the story and follow along at the listening center. (Tape the story for children to follow along.)
10. List important words from each big book.
11. Have children make their own collection of big book words that they can store in file boxes or rings.
12. Print the story text on paper, leaving a very large blank space at the top of the page. Have individual students or groups illustrate each page.
13. Rewrite the story in a different way using the same pattern.
14. Have students make their own big books.

The two largest big book makers in the United States are the Wright Group (10949 Technology Place, San Diego, CA 92127) and Scholastic Books (P. O. Box 7501, Jefferson City, MO 65102).

The Writing Process

Second and third graders can be active learners through the writing process (15). This approach relies on a five-step procedure that consists of rehearsing (brainstorming), drafting, revising, editing, and publishing. Second grade teacher Linda Gurosky has developed a management system for the writing process with the following rules:

1. No story starters are provided. Children are encouraged to think of their own topics and write about them.

2. Every child writes at a set time for 30 minutes a day using rehearsing, drafting, revising, and editing.

3. The teacher holds daily conferences. With 25 children in the class, five are assigned as Monday children, five as Tuesday children, and so forth.

4. Monday children have the opportunity to share with the class on Monday while Tuesday children share on Tuesday. This sharing time is optional and occurs after the 30-minute writing period.

5. Rehearsing, drafting, revising, and editing all occur three weeks out of each month. The last week of every month is reserved for publishing. Publishing refers to binding a story into a book or booklet.

6. A child is free to choose the writing he or she wishes to publish. The teacher helps with the editing but the choice of topics is left up to the students' judgments. (16)

ACTIVITY-ORIENTED MATHEMATICS

Since children move from concrete to semiconcrete to abstract concepts, the early childhood classroom and the math center should be activity-oriented and full of manipulatives. These manipulatives can be teacher-made, teacher-gathered, or commercially produced (31). Manipulative materials that should be in the math center include the following:

Teacher-Made Materials

felt shapes	felt board
numeral index cards	sandpaper numerals
gameboards	clock face

Teacher-Collected Materials

carpet squares	dried beans
washers	egg cartons
containers of various sizes	playing cards
bottle caps	string
ribbon	yarn
clocks	

Commercially Produced Materials

play money	sand timer
rulers	meter sticks
yardsticks	number/shape puzzles
lotto games	dominoes
abacus	Cuisenaire rods
unit blocks	pegs and pegboards
one-inch cubes	

Children in activity-based classes construct knowledge about mathematics from daily living situations and games (22). Daily living situations lend themselves to math concepts. Some of the ways children learn math through daily situations are by taking attendance, distributing things, returning library books, collecting permission slips, making calendars, talking about time, discussing ages, planning a party and counting gameboard pieces. Teachers in activity-focused classes seize every opportunity to turn practical life events into active math lessons.

Games are a major part of activity math. Concepts that are easily approached and learned through games include classifying, matching, sets, working with base ten (place value), addition, subtraction multiplication, division, investigating length, examining weight, measurement, time, geometry, and money (31). An example of an activity game is provided for each concept.

Classification

Game Name: Bean Buddies
Materials: A large container with a variety of beans
Procedure: Have students match the beans that go together (that look alike). The activity can be extended by having them count the number of beans in each pile.

Matching

Game Name: Double Decker
Materials: Two identical decks of playing cards
Procedure: Have one or two children match the playing cards of one deck with those of the other.

Sets

Game Name: Snack Math
Materials: Napkins, cookies, cups, spoons, plates
Procedure: Have one or two students match one of each item in the materials section to be distributed during snack time.

Working with Base Ten (or Place Value)

Game Name: Clothespin Base Ten
Materials: Cut two rectangles from sturdy cardboard and fold each piece twice. Place the word "tens" on one piece and "ones" on the other. Use clothespins of two different colors (one color for the tens and another for the ones).
Procedure: Show children numerals from one to 100. Have them place the right number of clothespins on the tens cardboard and the right number on the ones cardboard.

Addition, Subtraction, Multiplication, and Division

Game Name: Dice Race
Materials: Number dice and game board
Procedure: Two to four children play this board game by taking turns rolling the dice. Each child has to add (or subtract or multiply or divide) the numbers he/she rolled and move the appropriate number of spaces on the game board.

Investigating Length

Game Name: Measuring Me
Materials: Long rolls of white butcher paper, rulers
Procedure: Children are paired to trace each other on a large piece of paper. Then they use rulers to measure their own features on their profile.

Examining Weight

Game Name: Pound for Pound
Materials: Pan balance, marbles, nuts, beans, blocks, washers, etc.
Procedure: Two children work together to see how many marbles weigh the same as so many beans.

Measurement Concepts

Game Name: Recipe Round-Up
Materials: Recipes from the art section of this chapter written in rebus
Procedure: Students follow the recipe measurement ingredients in preparing the paste, playdough, etc.

Time Concepts

Game Name: Sand Timer Tester

Materials: Sand timer (minute)

Procedure: Students work in pairs. Partners think of an activity to ask each other to perform. Each one tries to complete the activity before the timer runs out.

Geometry

Game Name: Shape People

Materials: Geometric templates in the shape of circles, triangles, squares, rectangles, diamonds, trapezoids, octagons, and others

Procedure: Children see how many figures (people, houses, animals, etc.) they can make by completing drawings using the templates.

Money

Game Name: Shopping Spree

Materials: Play money, a page of ads from the newspaper

Procedure: Students work in pairs. Give each child a set amount of money. The child then chooses what he/she wants to buy from his/her page of advertisements. The partner helps add up the purchases and serves as the clerk to give correct change. Roles are then changed.

ACTIVITY-ORIENTED SCIENCE

There are three basic science areas that young children need to explore: living things, the planets, and energy and matter (31). These three areas can be approached through the scientific process of observing, classifying, hypothesizing, experimenting, communicating, and interpreting or generalizing (31). Several examples of activities for each of the science areas follow.

60

Living Things

Activity Name: Seed Watching
Materials: Large bean seeds, container of water
Procedure: Children soak the bean seeds in water and leave them overnight. They predict what they will find inside the seeds when they open them the following day.

Activity Name: Animal Categories
Materials: Large poster board and markers
Procedures: Have children develop charts of common animal categories. They may start with something simple, such as animals with no legs, with two legs, four legs, six legs, eight legs, and more than eight legs. Older children can classify the animals into amphibians, reptiles, etc. Children draw or cut out pictures from magazines to place under the appropriate category on the chart.

Activity Name: Insect Travel
Materials: Caterpillars, beetles, ants, walking sticks, baking soda
Procedure: Lightly dust the table top working surface with baking soda. Place a caterpillar on the surface. Have children chart the path the caterpillar takes, using a pencil. They can repeat this with the beetle and other insects.

The Planets (Earth)

Activity Name: Rock Time
Materials: Rocks and books about rocks
Procedure: Students make a rock collection and classify the rocks in some way. They discuss how they classified them.

Activity Name: Pinwheels
Materials: Paper squares, drinking straws, stick pins, small fan
Procedure: Students make a pinwheel. Then they use a fan, blow on the pinwheel, or go outside to observe the effects of the wind on the pinwheel.

Energy and Matter

Activity Name: Float or Sink
Materials: Large bowl of water, various objects (some that float, some that do not)
Procedure: Students work in pairs to observe, classify, communicate, and generalize about the items that floated and those that did not.

Activity Name: What's the Matter?
Materials: Ice cubes
Procedure: Students take two identical ice cubes and weigh them. (They should be as close to the same weight as possible.) Place one ice cube back in the freezer and put the other in a sealed plastic bag. After the ice cube in the plastic bag has melted, remove the ice cube from the freezer and weigh both the ice cube and the water in the plastic bag separately and together. Have students discuss what happened.

ACTIVITY-ORIENTED SOCIAL STUDIES

Children in activity-based social studies learn about (1) themselves and their families, (2) people and society, (3) customs and traditions. As children learn about families, society, and culture, they can begin to develop knowledge about anthropology, history, psychology, geography, ecology, sociology, political science, and economics. Three examples of activities for each of the three basic social science areas follow (30).

Understanding Family and Self

Activity Name: My Family Collage

Materials: Paper, markers or crayons, magazines

Procedure: All students draw or clip from magazines pictures to prepare a collage about themselves. The collage can represent family members, pets, favorite things to do, favorite things to eat, and vacations or places visited.

Activity Name: Talent Time

Materials: Media or instruments necessary for sharing talents

Procedure: Ask individuals or groups of children to share with the class something they enjoy doing.

Activity Name: Family Tree

Materials: Chart paper and markers

Procedure: Demonstrate how to make a family tree by constructing your family tree. Children then make their family trees.

Activity Name:	Neighborhood Map
Materials:	Markers, construction paper, poster board, rulers
Procedure:	Show children how to make a neighborhood map by constructing a map of the immediate school neighborhood with them. Children then make a map of their neighborhood or the route they travel to school.

Activity Name:	Buried Treasure Map
Materials:	Paper, pencil, shovel
Procedure:	This activity shows children how people use maps. A small group of children hides several "treasures" on the playground and then makes a hidden treasure map. Other children are provided a copy of the map and must find the buried treasure using the map.

Activity Name:	Classroom Reported News
Materials:	Paper, pencil, pretend microphones
Procedure:	Each week appoint two children as classroom reporters and two others as newscasters. The reporters collect information about the class members, write their reports, and present them to the newscasters. The newscasters must present the news to the rest of the class.

Understanding Customs and Traditions

Activity Name:	Native American Helpers
Materials:	Books and resources about Native Americans
Procedure:	Children search for Native American contributions in foods, clothing, furniture, and other areas. They make a chart of all the contributions they can find.
Activity Name:	Folktales from Other Friends
Materials:	Selected folktales from other countries
Procedure:	Read folktales from other cultures to children. Have them act out a foreign folktale and then write their own folktales.
Activity Name:	Foods from Foreign Friends
Materials:	Recipes from other countries
Procedure:	Children help prepare and eat foods that are customary for other nations.

Chapter 6

CONCLUSION

The activities presented in the preceding chapters have been tried by teachers in many different schools and have been found to be extremely effective with children. Nevertheless, it is important to remember that the activities given here are only illustrative of many more that teachers can devise for the unique children in their classrooms. Planning sessions that focus on developing activities for specific classrooms and children are fun and challenging for colleagues who find that collaboration makes the old adage "Two heads are better than one" come true.

When the curriculum for the kindergarten and primary grades is activity-oriented, teachers are devising environments that tap the child's sensory and psychological frameworks. The learner is able to use his/her judgment, solve problems, make choices among many interesting activities that are available, and therefore learn the value of making wise decisions—all of which facilitate more autonomous learning.

In addition, activities that encourage interaction of materials with a child's mind promote curiosity and imaginative explorations that are normally not as possible when only written words or pictures or verbal explanations or single demonstrations are used one at a time. Discovering, finding solutions, creating meaning, and working with other children in small-group situations facilitate cognitive, language, and social development simultaneously. Also, in such an environment, children feel better about themselves in situations in which they are not frustrated and are able to know that they can be successful. Through the use of multilevel activities, the curriculum is then geared to each child's experiential background and developmental level. Many "canned" and published programs are designed specifically for children to fit them or fail. With such an expectation, the emphasis is far overweighted toward the curriculum rather than toward the child interacting with the curriculum.

With appropriate activities and teacher support of children's efforts, the curriculum can be planned and implemented through self-pacing on the part of learners. Then the knowledge gained by educators through the years can be used and the classroom environment can become a laboratory where ideas, books, experiments, questions, observations, touching, tasting, feeling textures, talking, listening, answering, "fooling around," creating, imagining, supporting, producing, building—are a part of every day.

The organization for learning activities can be subservient to that of children and teacher supporting a curriculum that is developed for each child's unique level. Studies more than 50-years-old began to show that the form of grouping was not nearly as important as the children's and teachers' attitudes toward the situation (28). Competent and conscientious teachers organize the day to facilitate freedom to learn.

Evaluation thus can consist of keeping samples of students' work over time and showing both children and parents the improvement that occurs over time. Portfolios can contain children's views of their work; samples of their work (including art, music, and teacher-made descriptions of various productions too large to keep in a portfolio); photographs; and parents' reactions to these products. Most of all, evaluation should begin with strengths and be devised to show improvement made. Almost everyone prospers by moving from strengths rather than from weaknesses. When we are viewed in relation to what we can do, it is easier to move into the areas where we need to take small steps to move forward. Also, it is important to try to have an evaluation mode that considers each individual in relation to himself/herself rather than to use artificial standards established by norm-referenced tests. When students become old enough to understand comparisons, then perhaps the school might use such methods. One thing is clear: before an individual has a fully developed self-concept and is able to think abstractly, school practices that compare children are inappropriate. Very few people develop abstract thinking abilities before ages 12 to 14; just when the self-concept is fully developed remains to be discovered—but certainly not before adulthood.

While one of the ultimate goals of schooling is now most often defined as "developing thinking skills," if activities at children's appropriate developmental levels are planned and presented, and if the learners have the opportunity to discuss their specific actions and the solutions arrived at with other children and adults, there is no better known way for developing both thinking skills and self-concept. The conventional wisdom in the child development literature remains that children learn through *their own actions* on objects and ideas and through meaningful interactions with others.

The NEA Professional Library has published extensively in the areas of thinking skills—for example: *Thinking Skills Instruction: Concepts and Techniques* (19), *Teaching Thinking Skills: English/Language Arts* (21), *Teaching Thinking Skills: Mathematics* (18), *Teaching Thinking Skills: Science* (27), *Teaching Thinking Skills: Social Studies* (29). Also, it has been a standard bearer in practices that enhance the self-concept. *Developing Positive Student Self-Concept* (32) is widely accepted. These materials, and others, help validate the basic notions and activities presented in previous chapters and should be reviewed to enhance those ideas.

In the long run, warm, supportive people who strive to develop safe, secure places for children and adults are the ones to assist children in best preparing for their future. These are the teachers who never will know the extent to which their influence has been felt, but who do know that their work makes them feel fulfilled.

APPENDIX

LIST OF PREDICTABLE BOOKS

The Animal. Lorna Balian. Nashville, Tenn.: Abingdon Press, 1972.

The Ants Go Marching. B. Freschet. New York: Charles Scribner's Sons, 1973.

Are You My Mother? P. D. Eastman. Don Mills, Ont.: William Collins Sons, 1960.

Brown Bear, Brown Bear. Bill Martin. New York: Holt, Rinehart and Winston, 1970.

The Bus Ride. Illustrated by J. Wager. Glenview, Ill: Scott, Foresman, 1971.

Catch a Little Fox. Beatrice de Regniers. New York: Seabury Press, 1970.

Chicken Soup with Rice. Maurice Sendak. New York: Harper, 1962.

Crocodile and Hen. Joan Lenax. New York: Harper and Row, 1969.

Drummer Hoff Adapted. Barbara Emberley. Illustrated by Ed Emberley. Englewood Cliffs, N.J.: Prentice-Hall, 1967.

Each Peach, Pear Plum. J. Allenberg, and A. Allenberg. New York: Viking Press, 1978.

Elephant in a Well. Marie Hall Ets. New York: Viking Press, 1972.

The Fat Cat. Jack Kent. New York: Scholastic, 1971.

Fire! Fire! Said Mrs. McGuire. Bill Martin. New York: Holt, Rinehart and Winston, 1970.

Flower Pot Is Not a Hat. Martha Moffett. New York: E. P. Dutton, 1972.

Fortunately. Remy Charlip. New York: Four Winds Press, 1964.

Frog Went A-Courtin'. John Langstaff. New York: Harcourt Brace Jovanovich, 1955.

Go Tell Aunt Rhody. Aliki. New York: Macmillan, 1974.

Goodnight Moon. Margaret Wise Brown. New York: Harper and Row, 1947.

Goodnight Owl. Pat Hutchins. New York: Macmillan, 1972.

The Great Big Enormous Turnip. A. Tolstoy. New York: Franklin Watts, 1968.

The Grouchy Lady Bug. Eric Carle. New York: Thomas Y. Crowell, 1977.

The Haunted House. Bill Martin. New York: Holt, Rinehart and Winston, 1970.

House Is a House for Me. Mary Ann Hoberman. New York: Viking Press, 1978.

Hush, Little Baby. Margot Zemach, New York: E. P. Dutton, 1976.

I Know an Old Lady Who Swallowed a Fly. Nadine Bernard Wescott. Boston: Little, Brown, 1980.

I Love Ladybugs. R. Van Allen. Allen, Tex.: DLM Teaching Resources, 1985.

I Once Knew a Man. F. Brandenberg. New York: Macmillan, 1970.

I Was Walking Down the Road. Sarah Barahas. New York: Scholastic, 1975.

It Looked Like Spilt Milk. Charles Shaw. New York: Harper and Row, 1947.

Just for You. Mercer Mayer. New York: Golden Books, 1975.

Just Like Daddy. Frank Asch. Englewood Cliffs, N.J.: Prentice-Hall, 1981.

King Rooster, Queen Hen. Anita Lobel. New York: Greenwillow Books 1975.

Klippety Klop. Ed Emberley. Boston: Little, Brown, 1974.

The Little Red Hen. Paul Galdone. New York: Scholastic 1973.

May I Bring a Friend? Beatrice de Regniers. New York: Atheneum, 1974.

Monkey Face. Frank Asch. New York: Parents Magazine Press, 1977.

Mother, Mother I Want Another. Maria Polushkin. New York: Crown, 1978.

The Napping House. Audrey Wood, and Don Wood. New York: Harcourt Brace Jovanovich, 1984.

Oh, A-Hunting We Will Go. John Langstaff. New York: Atheneum, 1974.

One Monday Morning. Uri Shulevitz. New York: Charles Scribner's Sons, 1967.

One, Two, Three, Goes the Sea. Alain. New York: Scholastic, 1964.

Over in the Meadow. Ezra Jack Keats. New York: Scholastic, 1971.

Rain Makes Applesauce. J. Scheer, and M. Bileck. New York: Holiday House, 1964.

The Rose in My Garden. Arnold Lobel. New York: Scholastic, 1984.

Rosie's Walk. Pat Hutchens. New York: Macmillan, 1968.

Rum Pum Pum. Maggie Duff. New York: Macmillan, 1978.

Seven Little Rabbits. John Becker. New York: Scholastic, 1973.

She'll Be Comin' Round the Mountain. Robert Quackenbush. Philadelphia: J. B. Lippincott, 1973.

Skip to My Lou. Robert Quackenbush. Philadelphia: J. B. Lippincott, 1975.

The Snow Child. F. Littledale. New York: Scholastic, 1978.

Someone Is Eating the Sun. Ruth Sonneborn. New York: Random House, 1974.

The Teeny Tiny Woman. Margot Zemach. New York: Scholastic, 1965.

Ten Little Animals. Carl Memling. New York: Golden Books, 1961.

Ten, Nine, Eight. M. Baug. New York: William Morrow, 1983.

The Three Billy Goats Gruff. Marcia Brown. New York: Harcourt Brace Jovanovich, 1957.

The Three Little Pigs. P. Geldone. New York: Seabury Press, 1970.

Titch. Pat Hutchens. New York: Collier Books, 1971.

Too Much Noise. A. McGovern. New York: Scholastic, 1967.

Treeful of Pigs. Arnold Lobel. New York: Greenwillow Books, 1979.

Turtle Tale. F. Asch. New York: Dial Press, 1978.

Twelve Days of Christmas. Brian Wildsmith. New York: Franklin Watts, 1972.

Upside Down Day. Julian Scheer, and Marvin Bileck. New York: Holiday House, 1968.

The Very Busy Spider. Eric Carle. New York: Philomel Books, 1984.

The Very Hungry Caterpillar. Eric Carle. New York: Philomel Books, 1981.

The Visit. Diane Wolkstein. New York: Alfred A. Knopf, 1977.

We're Off to Catch a Dragon. Ester Laurence. Nashville, Tenn.: Abingdon Press, 1969.

What Do You Do with a Kangaroo? Mercer Mayer. New York: Scholastic, 1973.

When I First Came to This Land. Oscar Brand. New York: Putnam's Sons, 1974.

Where Did My Mother Go? Edna Mitchell Preston. New York: Four Winds Press, 1978.

Whose Mouse Are You? Robert Kraus. New York: Collier Books, 1970.

Why Can't I Fly? R. Gelman. New York: Scholastic, 1976.

Source: Maryann Manning, Gary Manning, Roberta Long, and Bernice Wolfson. *Reading and Writing in the Primary Grades.* Washington, D.C.: National Education Association, 1987.

BIBLIOGRAPHY

1. Aldridge, Jerry. "Helping Children Build Self-Esteem." *Day Care and Early Education* 17, no. 2 (Winter 1989): 4-7.

2. _____ . "Individualizing for Language Arts." In *Mainstreaming: A Practical Approach for Teachers*, edited by Judy W. Wood. Columbus, Ohio: Charles E. Merrill Publishing Co., 1989.

3. Aldridge, Jerry, and Cowles, Milly. "The Development of Significance in Students Through the Acceptance of Personality, Cognitive and Language Differences." *Education* 110, no. 3 (Spring 1990): 323-25.

4. Aldridge, Jerry, and Rust, Debra. "Young Children Teach Themselves to Read and Write." *Day Care and Early Education* 15, no. 2 (Winter 1987): 29-31.

5. Allen, Roach Van. *Language Experiences in Communication.* Boston: Houghton Mifflin, 1976.

6. Bredekamp, Sue. *Developmentally Appropriate Practice in Early Childhood Programs Serving Children from Birth Through Age 8.* Washington, D.C.: National Association for the Education of Young Children, 1987.

7. Bronfenbrenner, Urie. "Ecology of the Family as a Context for Human Development: Research Perspectives." *Developmental Psychology* 22, no. 6 (1986): 723-42.

8. Cloer, Thomas; Aldridge, Jerry; and Dean, Rose M. "Examining Different Levels of Print Awareness." *Journal of Language Experience* 4, nos. 1 and 2 (1981/1982): 25-33.

9. Cowles, Milly. *Quality Early Childhood Education in the South.* Decatur, Ga.: Commission on Elementary Schools, Southern Association of Colleges and Schools, 1990.

10. Croft, Doreen J. *An Activities Handbook for Teachers of Young Children.* Boston: Houghton Mifflin, 1990.

11. Dunn, Rita; Beaudry, Jeffrey; and Klavas, Angela. "Survey of Research on Learning Styles." *Educational Leadership* 47, no. 5 (March 1989): 50-58.

12. Eddowes, E. Anne, and Aldridge, Jerry. "Hyperactive or 'Activity Hyper': Helping Young Children Attend in Appropriate Environments." *Day Care and Early Education* 17, no. 4 (Summer 1990): 29-32.

13. Elkind, David. "Developmentally Appropriate Practice: Philosophical and Practical Implications." *Phi Delta Kappan* (October 1989): 114-17.

14. Gardner, Howard. *Frames of Mind: The Theory of Multiple Intelligences.* New York: Basic Books, 1983.

15. Graves, Donald. *Writing: Teachers and Children at Work.* Portsmouth, N.H.: Heinemann Educational Books, 1983.

16. Gurosky, Linda. "A Second Grader's Revision: One Part of the Writing Process." Paper presented at the 15th annual meeting of the Mid-South Educational Research Association, Memphis, Tenn., 1986.

17. Harris, Joey, and Aldridge, Jerry. "3 for Me is Better than 2 for You." *Academic Therapy* 18, no. 3 (January 1983): 361-64.

18. Heiman, Marcia; Narode, Ronald; Slomianko, Joshua; and Lochhead, Jack. *Teaching Thinking Skills: Mathematics.* Washington, D.C.: National Education Association,1987.

19. Heiman, Marcia, and Slomianko, Joshua, eds. *Thinking Skills Instruction: Concepts and Techniques.* Washington, D.C.: National Education Association, 1987.

20. Holdaway, Don. *The Foundations of Literacy.* Exeter, N.H.: Heinemann Educational Books, 1979.

21. Jones, Beau Fly: Tinzmann, Margaret B.; Friedman, Lawrence, B.; and Walker, Beverly Butler. *Teaching Thinking Skills: English/ Language Arts.* Washington, D.C.: National Education Association, 1987.

22. Kamii, Constance. *Young Children Reinvent Arithmetic: Implications of Piaget's Theory.* New York: Teachers College Press, 1985.

23. Katz, Lilian; Evangelou, Demetra; and Hartman, Jeanette. *The Case for Mixed-Age Grouping in Early Education.* Washington, D.C.: National Association for the Education of Young Children, 1990.

24. Manning, Maryann; Manning, Gary; Long, Roberta; and Wolfson, Bernice. *Reading and Writing in the Primary Grades.* Washington, D.C.: National Education Association, 1987.

25. Matthes, Carole. *How Children Are Taught to Read.* Lincoln, Neb.: Professional Educators Publications, 1977.

26. McClure, Ann. "Predictable Books: Another Way to Teach Reading to Learning Disabled Children." *Teaching Exceptional Children* 17, no. 4 (1985): 267-73.

27. Narode, Ronald; Heiman, Marcia; Lochhead, Jack; and Slomianko, Joshua. *Teaching Thinking Skills: Science.* Washington, D.C.: National Education Association, 1987.

28. Reed, Katherine, and Patterson, June. *The Nursery School and Kindergarten: Human Relations and Learning.* New York: Holt, Rinehart and Winston, 1980.

29. Rosenblum-Calé, Karen. *Teaching Thinking Skills: Social Studies.* Washington, D.C.: National Education Association, 1987.

30. Safford, Philip. *Integrated Teaching in Early Childhood: Starting in the Mainstream.* White Plains, N.Y.: Longman, 1989.

31. Schickedanz, Judith A.; York, Mary E.; Stewart, Ida Santos; and White, Doris A. *Strategies for Teaching Young Children.* 2d ed. Englewood Cliffs, N.J.: Prentice Hall, 1983.

32. Silvernail, David L. *Developing Positive Student Self-Concept.* 2d ed. Washington, D.C.: National Education Association, 1987.

33. Veatch, Jeanette; Sawicki, F.; Elliott, G.; Barnette, E.; and Blakey, J. *Key Words to Reading: The Language Experience Approach Begins.* Columbus, Ohio: Merrill, 1979.

34. Wadsworth, Barry. *Piaget's Theory of Cognitive and Affective Development.* White Plains, N.Y.: Longman, 1990.

35. Waynant, Louise, and Wilson, Robert. *Learning Centers: A Guide for Effective Use.* Paoli, Pa.: Instructo Corp., 1974.